THE SONG OF THE BIRD

*The books of Father Anthony de Mello
were written in a multi-religious
context to help the followers of other
religions, agnostics and atheists in
their spiritual search, and they were
not intended by the author as manuals
of instruction of the catholic faithful in
christian doctrine or dogma.*

Anthony de Mello S.J.

THE SONG
OF THE BIRD

2006
GUJARAT SAHITYA PRAKASH
P.B.70, ANAND – 388001
GUJARAT, INDIA.

1st Edition 1981
20th Edition 2006

ISBN 81-87886-20-X

Price: Rs. 70.00; US$ 9.00

Published by K.T. Mathew, S.J., Gujarat Sahitya Prakash
P.B.. 70, Anand, Gujarat, 388 001, India.
Laser-set and Printed by Agnelo Vaz, S.J., Anand Press, P.B. 95
Gamdi-Anand, Gujarat, 388 001, India.

CONTENTS

	Page
Eat your own fruit	1
A vital difference	2
The song of the bird	3
The sting	4
The elephant and the rat	5
The royal pigeon	6
Monkey salvation for a fish	7
Salt and cotton in the river	8
The search for the ass	9
True spirituality	10
The little fish	12
Did you hear that bird sing?	14
I chop wood	16
The bamboos	18
Constant awareness	20
Holiness in the present moment	22
The temple bells	23
The Word made flesh	25
The man idol	26
Searching in the wrong place	27
The question	28
Label makers	29
The formula	31
The explorer	32
Thomas Aquinas stops writing	33
The smarting dervish	34
One note of wisdom	35

What are you saying?   36
The devil and his friend   38
Nasruddin is dead   39
Bones to test our faith   41
Why good people die   42
The master does not know   43
Look into his eyes   44
Wheat from Egyptian tombs   46
Amend the Scriptures   47
The blind man's wife   48
The professionals   49
The experts   50
The soup of the soup of the duck   51
The monster in the river   52
The poisoned arrow   53
The baby stops crying   55
The egg   57
Shout to keep safe   58
River water for sale   59
The medal   60
Nasruddin in China   61
Liturgical vestments   62
Dandelions   64
Don't change   66
My friend   68
The Arab aspirant   70
We are three, you are three   71
Prayer can be dangerous   73
Narada   74
Destiny in a tossed coin   76
Praying for rain   77
The disabled fox   78
The food god   79
The five monks   80
The job   81
Diogenes   82

Stand up and be counted 84
The truth shop 85
The narrow path 86
The phony 88
The dream contract 89
Very well, very well 91
Sons dead in a dream 92
The golden eagle 93
The duckling 94
The salt doll 95
Who am I? 96
The talkative lover 97
Dropping the 'I' 98
Drop your nothing 99
The Zen master and the Christian 100
Comfort for the devil 102
Better sleep than slander 103
The monk and the woman 104
The spiritual heart attack 105
To know Christ 106
The look of Jesus 108
The golden egg 109
The good news 110
Joneyed and the barber 112
The elder son 114
The old lady's religion 115
Love's forgetfulness 116
The lotus 117
The turtle 118
Bayazid breaks the rule 120
Streaky people 121
Music to the deaf 122
Riches 123
The contented fisherman 124
The seven jars of gold 126
A parable of modern life 128

Hofetz Chaim	129
The sky and the crow	130
Who can steal the moon?	131
The diamond	132
Pray for a contented mind	133
The World Fair of Religions	134
Discrimination	136
Jesus at the football match	137
Religious hatred	138
Offensive and defensive prayer	139
Ideology	140
Change the world by changing me	142
Domesticated rebels	143
The lost sheep	145
The perfect apple	146
The slave girl	147
Confucius the sage	149
O happy fault!	151
The coconut	152
The singer's voice fills the hall	153
Thanks and yes	155
Simon Peter	157
The Samaritan woman	158
Ignatius of Loyola	160

This book has been written for people of every persuasion, religious and non-religious. I cannot, however, hide from my readers the fact that I am a priest of the Catholic Church. I have wandered freely in mystical traditions that are not Christian and not religious and have been profoundly influenced by them. It is to my Church, however, that I keep returning, for she is my spiritual home; and while I am acutely, sometimes embarrassingly, conscious of her limitations and narrowness, I also know that it is she who has formed me and made me what I am today. So it is to her that I gratefully dedicate this book.

Everyone loves stories and you will find plenty of them in this book: Stories that are Buddhist, Christian, Zen, Hasidic, Russian, Chinese, Hindu, Sufi; stories ancient and contemporary.

And they all have a special quality: if read in a certain kind of way, they will produce spiritual growth.

HOW TO READ THEM

There are three ways:

1. Read a story once. Then move on to another. This manner of reading will give you entertainment.

2. Read a story twice. Reflect on it. Apply it to your life. That will give you a taste of theology. This sort of thing can be fruitfully done in a group where the members share their reflections on the story. You then have a theological circle.

3. Read the story again, after you have reflected on it. Create a silence within you and let the story reveal to you its inner depth and meaning: something beyond words and reflections. This will give you a feel for the mystical.

   Or carry the story around all day and allow its *fragrance,* its melody to haunt you. Let it speak to your heart, not to your brain. This too could make something of a mystic out of you. It is with this mystical end in view that most of these stories were originally told.

CAUTION

Most of the stories have a comment appended to them. The comment is meant to be a sample of the kind of comment you yourself may want to make. Make your own. Don't limit yourself to the ones you find in this book. Why borrow someone else's insights?

Beware of applying the story to anyone (priest, mullah, church, neighbour) other than yourself. If you do so the story will do you damage. Every one of these stories is about *you,* no one else.

When you read the book for the first time read the stories in the order in which they are set down here. The order imparts a teaching and a spirit which will be lost if the stories are read haphazardly.

GLOSSARY

Theology: The art of telling stories about the Divine. Also the art of listening to them.

Mysticism: The art of tasting and feeling in your heart the inner meaning of such stories to the point that they transform you.

EAT YOUR OWN FRUIT

A disciple once complained:
  "You tell us stories, but you never
  reveal their meaning to us."

Said the Master:
  "How would you like it if someone
  offered you fruit and masticated it
  before giving it to you?"

A VITAL DIFFERENCE

Uwais, the Sufi, was once asked:
"What has Grace brought you?"

He replied:
"When I wake in the morning I feel
like a man who is not sure he will
live till evening."

Said the questioner:
"But doesn't everyone know this?"

Said Uwais:
"They certainly do.
But not all of them
feel it."

No one ever became drunk on the word *wine*.

THE SONG OF THE BIRD

*The disciples were full of questions
about God.*

*Said the Master, "God is Unknown,
the Unknowable. Every statement about
Him, every answer to your questions,
is a distortion of the Truth."*

*The disciples were bewildered. "Then why
do you speak about Him at all?"*

"Why does the bird sing?" said the Master.

Not because he has a statement, but because he
has a song.

The words of the Scholar are to be understood. The
words of the Master are not to be understood. They
are to be listened to as one listens to the wind in
the trees and the sound of the river and the song of
the bird. They will awaken something within the
heart that is beyond all knowledge.

3

THE STING

*A saint was once given the gift of
speaking the language of the ants. He
approached one, who seemed the scholarly type,
and asked, "What is the Almighty like? Is he in
any way similar to the ant?"*

*Said the scholar, "The Almighty?
Certainly not! We ants, you see, have
only one sting. But the Almighty, he
has two!"*

Suggested post script:

When asked what heaven was like, the ant-scholar
solemnly replied, "There we shall be just like Him,
having two stings each, only smaller ones."

A bitter controversy rages among religious schools
of thought as to where exactly the second sting will
be located in the heavenly body of the ant.

THE ELEPHANT AND THE RAT

An elephant was enjoying a dip in a jungle pool when a rat came up to insist that he get out.

"I won't," said the elephant.

"I insist you get out this minute," said the rat.

"Why?"

"I shall tell you that only after you are out of the pool."

"Then I won't get out."

But he finally lumbered out of the pool, stood in front of the rat and said, "Now then, why did you want me to get out of the pool?"

"To check if you were wearing my swimming trunks," said the rat.

An elephant will sooner fit into the trunks of the rat than God into our notions of him.

THE ROYAL PIGEON

Nasruddin became prime minister to the king. Once while he wondered through the palace, he saw a royal falcon.

Now Nasruddin had never seen this kind of a pigeon before. So he got out a pair of scissors and trimmed the claws, the wings and the beak of the falcon.

"Now you look like a decent bird," he said. "Your keeper had evidently been neglecting you."

"You're different so there's something wrong with *you!*"

6

MONKEY SALVATION FOR A FISH

*"What on earth are you doing?" said I
to the monkey when I saw him lift a
fish from the water and place it
on a tree.*

*"I am saving it from drowning," was the
reply.*

The sun that gives sight to the eagle
blinds the owl.

SALT AND COTTON IN THE RIVER

Nasruddin was taking a load of salt
to the market. His donkey waded through
the river and the salt dissolved. When
it reached the opposite bank the animal
ran around in circles, overjoyed that
its load had been lightened. But Nasruddin was
annoyed.

On the next market day he packed the
panniers with cotton. The ass nearly
drowned with the increased weight of the
cotton socked in the river water.

"There!" said Nasruddin gleefully. "That
will teach you to think that each time
you go through water you stand to gain!"

Two persons walked into religion.
One came alive, the other drowned.

THE SEARCH FOR THE ASS

*Everyone became alarmed when they saw
Mulla Nasruddin mounted on his ass,
charging through the streets of the
village.*

*"Where are you off to, Mullah?" they
asked.*

*"I'm searching for my ass," said the
Mulla as he whizzed by.*

The Zen Master Rinzai was once seen searching
for his body. It provided endless entertainment to
his unenlightened disciples.

One even comes across people who say they are
searching for God!

TRUE SPIRITUALITY

The Master was asked, "What is Spirituality?"

He said, "Spirituality is that which succeeds in bringing one to Inner Transformation."

'But if I apply the traditional methods handed down by the Masters, is that not Spirituality?"

"It is not Spirituality if it does not perform its function for you. A blanket is no longer a blanket if it does not keep you warm."

"So Spirituality does change?"

"People change and needs change. So what was Spirituality once is Spirituality no more. What generally goes under the name of Spirituality is merely the record of past methods."

Don't cut the person to fit the coat.

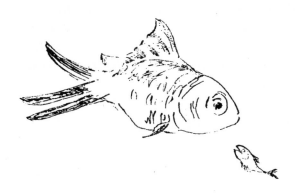

THE LITTLE FISH

"Excuse me," said an ocean fish,
"You are older than I so can
you tell me where to find this
thing they call the Ocean?"

"The Ocean," said the older fish, "is the thing
you are in now."

"Oh, this? But this is water. What I'm seeking is
the Ocean," said the disappointed fish as he
swam away to search elsewhere.

He came to the Master in sannyasi robes. And he
spoke sannyasi language: "For years I have been
seeking God. I have sought Him everywhere that
He is said to be: on mountain peaks, the vastness
of the desert, the silence of the cloister and the
dwellings of the poor."

"Have you found him?" the Master asked.

"No. I have not. Have you?"

What could the Master say? The evening sun was sending shafts of golden light into the room. Hundreds of sparrows were twittering on a banyan tree. In the distance one could hear the sound of highway traffic. A mosquito droned a warning that it was going to strike... And yet this man could sit there and say he had not found Him.

After a while he left, disappointed, to search elsewhere.

*   *   *   *   *   *   *

Stop searching, little fish. There isn't anything to look *for*. All you have to do is *look*.

DID YOU HEAR THAT BIRD SING?

Hindu India developed a magnificent image to describe God's relationship with Creation. God 'dances' Creation. He is the Dancer, Creation is his Dance. The dance is different from the dancer, yet it has no existence apart from him. You cannot take it home in a box, if it pleases you. The moment the dancer stops, the dance ceases to be.

In our quest for God, we think too much, reflect too much, talk too much. Even when we look at this dance that we call creation, we are the whole time thinking, talking, (to ourselves and others) reflecting, analysing, philosophizing. Words. Noise.

Be silent and contemplate the Dance. Just look: a star, a flower, a fading leaf, a bird, a stone... any fragment of the Dance will do. Look. Listen. Smell. Touch. Taste. And, hopefully, it won't be long before you see Him–the Dancer Himself!

The disciple was always complaining
to his Master, "You are hiding the
final secret of Zen from me." And
he would not accept the Master's denials.

One day they were walking in the hills
when they heard a bird sing.

"Did you hear that bird sing?"
said the Master.

"Yes," said the disciple.

"Well, now you know that I have hidden nothing from you."

"Yes."

If you really heard a bird sing, if you really saw a tree... you would know. Beyond words and concepts.

What was that you said? You have heard dozens of birds sing and seen hundreds of trees? Ah, was it the tree you saw or the label? If you look at a tree and see a tree, you have really not seen the tree. When you look at the tree and see a miracle–then, at last, you have seen! Did your heart never fill with wordless wonder when you heard a bird in song?

I CHOP WOOD!

When the Zen Master attained Enlightenment
he wrote the following lines to celebrate it:

"Oh wondrous marvel:
I chop wood!
I draw water from the well!"

After enlightenment nothing really changes. The tree is still a tree; people are just what they were before; and so are you. You may continue to be as moody or even-tempered, as wise or foolish. The one difference is that you see things with a different eye. You are more detached from it all now. And your heart is full of wonder.

16

That is the essence of Contemplation: the Sense of Wonder.

Contemplation is different from ecstasy in that ecstasy leads to withdrawal. The enlightened contemplative continues to chop wood and draw water from the well. Contemplation is different from the perception of beauty in that the perception of beauty (a painting or a sunset) produces aesthetic delight, whereas contemplation produces wonder— no matter what it observes, a sunset or a stone.

This is the prerogative of children. They are often in a state of wonder. So they easily slip into the Kingdom.

THE BAMBOOS

Brownie, our dog, sat looking up the tree, ears cocked, tail tensely wagging. He was attending to a monkey. Just one thing filled his consciousness: the monkey. No thought disturbed his total concentration, no worry for tomorrow. Brownie was the nearest thing to Contemplation I have ever seen.

You may have experienced some of this yourself when you were totally absorbed watching a cat at play.

Here is a formula for Contemplation, as good as any I know: Be totally in the present. Drop every thought of the future, drop every thought of the past, drop every image and abstraction, and come into the present. Contemplation will arise!

After years of training, the disciple
begged his Master to bring him to
Enlightenment. The Master led him
to a bamboo grove and said, "See
that bamboo, how tall it is? See
that other one there, how short it is?"
And the disciple was enlightened.

They say Buddha practised every form of asceticism known to the India of his times, in an effort to attain enlightenment. In vain. One day he sat under a bodhi tree and enlightenment occurred. He passed on the secret of enlightenment to his disciples in words that must seem strange to the uninitiated: "When you draw in a deep breath, oh monks, be aware that you are drawing in a deep breath. And when you draw in a shallow breath, oh monks, be aware that you are drawing in a shallow breath. And when you draw in a medium-sized breath, oh monks, be aware that you are drawing in a medium-sized breath." Awareness. Attention. Absorption.

This kind of absorption one sees in little children. They are close to the Kingdom.

19

CONSTANT AWARENESS

*No Zen student would presume to teach
others till he had lived with his
Master for a minimum of ten years.*

*Tenno, having completed his ten years
of apprenticeship, acquired the rank of teacher.
One day he went to visit the Master Nan-in. It
was a rainy day, so Tenno wore wooden clogs
and carried an umbrella.*

*When he walked in, Nan-in greeted him
with, "You left your wooden clogs
and umbrella on the porch, didn't
you? Tell me, did you place your
umbrella on the right side of the
clogs or on the left?"*

*Tenno was embarrassed, for he did not know
the answer. He realized he lacked
Awareness. So he became Nan-in's student
and laboured for ten more years
to acquire Continual Awareness.*

The person who is ceaselessly aware: the person
who is totally there each moment: behold the
Master!

HOLINESS IN THE PRESENT MOMENT

Buddha was once asked, "What makes a person holy?" He replied, "Every hour is divided into a certain number of seconds and every second into a certain number of fractions. Anyone who is able to be totally present in each fraction of a second is holy."

The Japanese warrior was captured and thrown into prison. At night he could not sleep for he was convinced he would be tortured next morning.

Then the words of his Master came to him: "Tomorrow is not real. The only reality is now."

So he came to the present – and fell asleep.

The person over whom the Future has lost its grip: How like the birds of the air and the lilies of the field. No anxieties for the morrow. Total presence in the now. Holiness!

THE TEMPLE BELLS

The temple was built on an island and it had a thousand bells. Bells big and small, fashioned by the finest craftsmen in the world. When the wind blew or a storm raged, all the bells would peal out in a symphony that would send the heart of the hearer into raptures.

But over the centuries the island sank into the ocean and, with it, the temple bells. An ancient legend said that the bells still rang out ceaselessly, and could be heard by anyone who would listen. Inspired by the legend a young man travelled thousands of miles, determined to hear those bells. He sat for days on the shore facing the vanished island and listened with all his might. But all he heard was the sound of the sea. He made every effort to block it out but to no avail; the sound of the sea seemed to flood the world.

He kept at his task for weeks. Each time he got disheartened he would listen to the village pundits as they spoke with unction of the mysterious legend. Then his heart would be

23

inflammed... only to become discouraged when weeks of further efforts yielded no results.

Finally he decided to give up the attempt. Perhaps he was not destined to listen to the bells. Perhaps the legend was not true. It was his final day, and he went to the shore to say goodbye to the sea and the sky and the wind and the coconut trees. He lay on the sand, and for the first time, listened to the sound of the sea.

Soon he was so lost in the sound that he was barely conscious of himself, so deep was the silence the sound produced.

In the depth of that silence, he heard it! The tinkle of a tiny bell followed by another, and another and another... till every one of the thousand temple bells was pealing out in harmony, and his heart was rapt in joyous ecstasy.

Do you wish to hear the temple bells? Listen to the sound of the sea.

Do you wish to catch a glimpse of God? Look intently at creation.

THE WORD MADE FLESH

In the Gospel of Saint John we read:

> *The Word became flesh; he came to dwell among us... through him all things came to be; no single thing was created without him. All that came to be was alive with his life, and that life was the light of men. The light shines on in the dark, and the darkness has never quenched it.*

Look steadily at the darkness. It won't be long before you see the light. Gaze at things. It won't be long before you see the Word.

> *The Word became flesh; he came to dwell among us...*

And stop those frantic efforts to change flesh back into words. Words, words, words!

25

THE MAN IDOL

An ancient Hindu story:

> *A shipwrecked merchant drifted to the shore of Sir Lanka where Vibhishana was the King of the Monsters. At the sight of him Vibhishana became ecstatic with joy and said, "Ah! He looks just like my Rama. The same human form!" He then had royal robes and jewels put on the merchant and worshipped him.*

The Hindu mystic, Ramakrishna, says, "When I first heard this story I felt an indescribable delight. If God can be worshipped in images of clay, should he not be worshipped in people?"

SEARCHING IN THE WRONG PLACE

A neighbour found Nasruddin on hands and knees.

"What are you searching for, Mullah?"

"My key."

Both men got on their knees to search. After a while the neighbour says, "Where did you lose it?"

"At home."

"Good Lord! Then why are you searching here?"

"Because it's brighter here."

Search for God where you lost Him.

THE QUESTION

*Said the monk, "All these mountains
and rivers and earth and stars—
where do they come from?"*

*Said the Master, "Where does
your question come from?"*

Search within!

LABEL MAKERS

Life is like heady wine.
Everyone reads the label on the bottle.
Hardly anyone tastes the wine.

*Buddha once pointed to a flower
and asked each of his disciples to
say something about it.*

*One pronounced a lecture.
Another a poem. Yet another
a parable. Each outdid the
other in depth and erudition.*

Label makers!

*Mahakashyap smiled and held his
tongue. Only he had seen the flower.*

If I could only *taste* a bird,
a flower,
a tree,
a human face!

But, alas, I have no time.
My energy is spent deciphering the label.

THE FORMULA

The mystic was back from the desert.
"Tell us," they said, "what God is like."

But how could he ever tell them
what he had experienced in his heart?
Can God be put into words?

He finally gave them a formula –
inaccurate, inadequate–in the hope
that some might be tempted
to experience it for themselves.

They seized upon the formula. They made it a
sacred text. They imposed it on others as a
holy belief. They went to great pains to spread
it in foreign lands. Some even gave their lives
for it.

The mystic was sad. It might have
been better if he had said nothing.

THE EXPLORER

The explorer returned to his people, who were eager to know about the Amazon. But how could he ever put into words the feelings that flooded his heart when he saw exotic flowers and heard the night-sounds of the forests; when he sensed the danger of wild beasts or paddled his canoe over treacherous rapids?

He said, "Go and find out for yourselves." To guide them he drew a map of the river. They pounced upon the map. They framed it in their Town Hall. They made copies of it for themselves. And all who had a copy considered themselves experts on the river, for did they not know its every turn and bend, how broad it was, how deep, where the rapids were and where the falls?

It is said that Buddha obdurately refused to be drawn into taking of God.

He was obviously familiar with the dangers of drawing maps for arm-chair explorers.

THOMAS AQUINAS STOPS WRITING

The story goes that one of the world's ablest theologians, Thomas Aquinas, suddenly stopped writing. When his secretary complained about his unfinished works, Thomas replied: 'Brother Reginald, some months ago I experienced something of the Absolute, so all I have ever written of God seems to me now to be like straw.'

How could it be otherwise when the scholar becomes a seer?

> *When the mystic came down from the mountain he was accosted by the atheist who said, sarcastically, "What did you bring us from that garden of delights you were in?"*
>
> *The mystic replied, "I had every intention of filling my skirt with flowers and giving them to my friends on my return. But while I was there I became so intoxicated with the fragrance of the garden that I let go of the skirt."*

The Zen Masters put it succinctly: "The one who knows, does not say. The one who says, does not know."

33

THE SMARTING DERVISH

*A dervish was sitting peacefully by a river
when a passerby saw the bare back of his
neck and yielded to the temptation to give it a
resounding whack. He was full of wonder at
the sound his hand had made on
the fleshy neck, but the dervish, smarting with
pain, got up to hit him back.*

*"Wait a minute," said the aggressor.
"You can hit me if you wish. But
answer this question first: Was the
sound of the whack produced by my
hand or by the back of your neck?"*

*Said the dervish, "Answer that yourself.
My pain won't allow me to theorize. You
can afford to do so, because you don't feel
what I feel."*

ONE NOTE OF WISDOM

No one knows what became of Kakua after he left the Emperor's presence. Here is the story:

Kakua was the first Japanese to study Zen in China. He had little use for travelling, for he took his meditation seriously. Whenever people found him out and invited him to preach, he would say a word or two and escape to another part of the forest where he would not be disturbed.

On his return to Japan the Emperor heard of him and commanded him to preach at court. Kakua stood silent and helpless before the King. Then he pulled out a flute from the folds of his robe, played one short note on it, bowed profoundly to the King and disappeared.

Confucius says: "Not teach ripe person: waste of person. Teach not ripe person: waste of words."

WHAT ARE YOU SAYING?

The Master imprints his wisdom in the heart of his disciple, not the pages of a book. The disciple might carry this wisdom in his heart for thirty or forty years, until he meets someone ready to receive it. Such was the tradition of Zen.

The Zen Master Mu-nan sent for his disciple Shoju one day and said, "I am an old man now, Shoju, and it is you who will carry on this teaching. Here is a book that has been handed down from Master to Master for seven generations. I have myself added some notes to it that you will find valuable. Here, keep it with you as a sign that I have made you my successor."

"You had better keep the book yourself," said Shoju. "I received your Zen without the help of

written words, and I am quite content to let it be that way."

"I know, I know," said Mu-nan patiently. "Even so, the book has served seven generations and may be helpful to you too. Here, keep it with you."

The two happened to be talking near the fire-place. The instant the book touched Shoju's hand he flung it into the fire. He had no lust for written words.

Mu-nan, who was never known to be angry before shouted, "You must be crazy! What are you doing?"

Shoju shouted back, "You are crazy yourself! What are you saying?"

THE DEVIL AND HIS FRIEND

The devil went for a walk with a friend.
Thew saw a man ahead of them stoop down
and pick up something from the ground.

"What did that man find?" asked the friend.

"A piece of Truth," said the devil.

"Doesn't that disturb you" asked the friend.

"No," said the devil, "I shall let him
make a belief out of it."

A religious belief is a signpost pointing the way to
Truth. When you cling to the signpost you are
prevented from moving towards the Truth because
you think you have it already.

NASRUDDIN IS DEAD

Nasruddin was in a philosophical frame of mind: "Life and Death–who can say what they are?" His wife looked up from her cooking and said, "You men are all like–unpractical. Anyone can tell that when a man's extremities are rigid and cold, he is dead."

Nasruddin was impressed by his wife's efficient wisdom. One day he was out in the snow when his hands and feet went numb. "I must be dead," he thought. Then came a further thought: "If I am dead, what am I doing walking about? I should be lying down like a normal corpse." Which is exactly what he did.

An hour later, a group of travellers, finding him by the roadside, fell to arguing among themselves about whether he was dead or alive. Nasruddin yearned to cry out, "Fools, can't you see my extremities are rigid and cold?" But he knew better than to say that, for corpses do not talk.

They finally concluded he was dead and put him on their shoulders to take him to the cemetery. They hadn't gone a mile when they came to a forking of the ways. A fresh dispute arose as to which road led to the burial ground. Nasruddin put up with this till he could take it no longer. Then he sat up and said: *"Excuse me, gentleman, but the road to the cemetery is the one to your left. I know that corpses do not speak, but I have broken the rule this once and I assure you it will not happen again."*

When Reality clashes with a rigidly held belief, Reality is generally the loser.

BONES TO TEST OUR FAITH

*A Christian scholar who held the Bible
to be literally true was once accosted
by a scientist who said, "According to the Bible
the earth was made five thousand years ago.
But we have discovered bones that point to
life on earth a million years ago."*

*Pat came the answer: "When God created
earth five thousand years ago, he deliberately
put those bones in to test our faith and see if
we would believe his Word rather than
scientific evidence."*

Further evidence of rigid belief leading to reality
distortion.

WHY GOOD PEOPLE DIE

The village preacher at the home of an elderly parishioner was busy answering grandma's questions over a cup of coffee.

"Why does the Lord send us epidemics every so often?" asked the old lady.

"Well," said the preacher, "sometimes people become so wicked they have to be removed and so the good Lord allows the coming of epidemics."

"But then," objected grandma, "why do so many good people get removed with the bad?"

"The good ones are summoned for witnesses," explained the preacher. "The Lord wants to give every soul a fair trial."

There is nothing that the Rigid Believer cannot find an explanation for.

THE MASTER DOES NOT KNOW

*The Seeker approached the Disciple
and asked respectfully, "What is
the meaning of human life?"*

*The Disciple consulted the Works of
his Master and confidently replied:
"Human life is nothing but the
expression of God's exuberance."*

*When the Seeker addressed the same
question to the Master himself, the
Master said, "I do not know."*

The Seeker says, "I do not know." That takes
honesty. The Master says, "I do not know." That
takes a mystic's mind that knows things through
non-knowing. The Disciple says, "I know." That
takes ignorance in the form of borrowed knowledge.

LOOK INTO HIS EYES

The Commander of the Occupation troops said to the Mayor of the mountain village. "We know you are hiding a traitor. Unless you give him up to us, we shall harass your people by every means in our power."

The village was, indeed, hiding a man who was evidently innocent. But what could the Mayor do now that the welfare of the village was at stake? Days of discussions in the Village Council led to no conclusion. So the Mayor took the matter up with the priest. Priest and Mayor spent a whole night searching the Scriptures and finally came up with a text that said, "It is better that one man die to save the nation."

So the Mayor handed over the fugitive whose screams echoed through the village as he was tortured till he died.

Twenty years later a prophet came to that village, went right up to that Mayor and said "How could you have done this? That man was sent by God to be the saviour of this country. And you handed him over to be tortured and killed."

*"But where did I go wrong?" the Mayor
pleaded. "The priest and I looked at the
Scriptures and did what they commanded."*

*"That's where you went wrong," said the
prophet. "You looked at the Scriptures. You
should have looked into his eyes."*

WHEAT FROM EGYPTIAN TOMBS

A handful of wheat, five thousand years old, was found in the tomb of one of the kings of ancient Egypt. Someone planted the grains and, to everyone's amazement, they came to life.

An enlightened person's words are like seeds of life and energy. They can remain in the form of seeds for centuries until they are sown in the fertile soil of a receptive heart.

I used to think the words of scripture dead and dry. But it was my heart that was barren and dead, so how could anything take root there?

AMEND THE SCRIPTURES

*Someone said to Buddha, "The things
you teach, sir, are not to be found
in Scripture."*

"Then put them there," said Buddha.

*After an embarrassed pause the man
went on to say, "May I dare to suggest,
sir, that some of the things
you teach actually contradict the
Scriptures?"*

*"Then the Scriptures need amending,"
said Buddha.*

A proposal was made at the United Nations that
the Scriptures of every religion be revised;
everything in them that leads to intolerance or
cruelty should be deleted; everything that damages
the dignity of human beings should be destroyed.

When it was found that the author of the proposal
was Jesus Christ, reporters rushed to his residence.
His explanation was simple: "Scripture, like the
Sabbath, is for human beings, not human beings
for Scripture."

THE BLIND MAN'S WIFE

*Someone married off his ugly daughter
to a blind man, for no one else would have her.*

*When a doctor offered to restore the blind
man's sight, the father of the girl would not
allow it, for he feared the man would repudiate
his daughter.*

Sa'di says about this tale, "The husband of an
ugly woman is best left blind."

And a defensive person ignorant.

THE PROFESSIONALS

My religious life has been taken over by professionals. To learn to pray I need a Spiritual Director; to find God's will for me I consult an Expert in Discernment; to understand the Bible I consult a Scripture Scholar; to know if I have sinned or not I need the Moral Theologian; and to have my sins forgiven I kneel before the Priest.

> *A native king in the South Sea Islands was hosting a banquet for a distinguished Western guest.*
>
> *When the time came to praise the guest, His Majesty remained seated on the floor while a professional orator, engaged for the occasion, eulogized the visitor.*
>
> *After the panegyric, the guest stood up to speak. His Majesty gently held him back. "No, no," he said, "I have hired an orator for you too. In our island we don't leave public speaking to amateurs."*

I wonder, would God appreciate it if I became more amateur in my relationship with Him?

THE EXPERTS

A Sufi tale:

A dead man suddenly came to life
and began to pound on the lid of the coffin.

The lid was raised; the man sat up.
"What are you doing?" he said to the
assembled crowd, "I am not dead."

His words were met with silent disbelief.
One of the mourners finally said,
"Friend, the doctors and the priests
have certified that you are dead.
So dead you are."

And he was duly buried.

THE SOUP OF THE SOUP OF THE DUCK

A relative came to visit Nasruddin bringing a duck as a gift. So the bird was cooked and eaten.

Soon a stream of guests began to call, each claiming to be a friend of the friend of the 'man who brought you the duck.' Each one, of course, expected to be fed and housed on the strength of that hapless bird.

The Mulla bore it manfully till the day a stranger arrived and said: "I am a friend of the friend of the kinsman who brought you the duck." And, like the others, he sat down, expecting to be fed.

Nasruddin placed a bowl of steaming water under his nose. "What's this?" asked the stranger.

"This," said the Mulla, "Is the soup of the soup of the duck that was brought me by your friend."

One hears of people who became the disciples of the disciples of someone who experienced the Divine.

How can you transmit a kiss through a messenger?

THE MONSTER IN THE RIVER

The village priest was distracted at his prayer by the children. To get rid of them he said, "Hurry to the river and you will see a monster breathing fire through his nostrils."

Soon the whole village had heard of this monstrous apparition and was rushing to the river. The priest too joined the crowd. As he panted his way through four solid miles, he kept saying to himself, "It is true I invented the story. But you never can tell!"

A good way to believe in the gods we have created is to convince others of their existence.

THE POISONED ARROW

*A monk once said to the Lord Buddha,
"Do the souls of the just survive death?"*

Characteristically, Buddha gave him no reply.

*But the monk persisted. Each day he would
repeat the question; and each day he would
get silence for an answer till he could take it no
more and threatened to quit unless this crucial
question was answered to his satisfaction, for
to what purpose was he living a life of
renunciation if the souls of the just perished
with their bodies?*

53

Then the Lord Buddha, in his compassion, spoke: "You are like a man," he said, "who was dying from a poisoned arrow. His relatives rushed a doctor to his side, but he refused to have the arrow taken out unless he had the answer to these three vital questions: First, was the man who shot him white or black? Second, was he tall or short? And third, was he a brahmin or an outcaste?"

The monk stayed on!

THE BABY STOPS CRYING

He claimed that, for all practical purposes, he had become an atheist. If he really thought for himself he would not believe the things his religion taught. The existence of God created more problems than it solved; life after death was a piece of wishful thinking; the scriptures and tradition had done as much harm as good. All these things were invented to soften the loneliness and despair of human life.

It was best to let him be. He was going through a stage of discovery and growth.

The Master was once asked by his disciple,
    "What is the Buddha?"
He replied,
    "The mind is the Buddha."

Another day, when asked the same question, he said,
    "No mind. No Buddha."

The disciple was confused:
    "But the other day you said, 'The mind is the Buddha."

Said the Master,
    "That was to stop the baby crying. When the baby stops crying, I say, 'No mind. No Buddha.'"

The baby in him had ceased to cry and he was ready for the truth. So it was best to let him be.

* * * * * * *

But when he started preaching his new-found atheism to those who weren't prepared for it, he had to be restrained: "There was a time when people adored the sun: the pre-scientific age. Then came the scientific age when they realized that the sun was not a god; it was not even a living thing. Finally came the age of mysticism when Francis of Assisi would call the sun his Brother and speak to it in reverential love."

"Your faith was that of a frightened child. Now that you have become fearless you have no need of it. Hopefully you will move on to the mystic stage and some day find your faith again."

* * * * * * *

Faith is the fearless search for truth.
So it is not lost when one questions one's beliefs.

THE EGG

*Nasruddin earned his living selling
eggs. Someone came to his shop one day
and said, "Guess what I have in my hand."*

"Give me a clue," said Nasruddin.

*"I shall give you several: It has
the shape of an egg, the size of an
egg. It looks like an egg, tastes
like an egg and smells like an egg.
Inside it is yellow and white. It is
liquid before it is cooked, becomes
thick when heated. It was, moreover
laid by a hen..."*

*"Aha! I know!" said Nasruddin. "It
is some kind of cake!"*

The expert misses the obvious!
The Chief Priest misses the Messiah!

SHOUT TO KEEP SAFE – AND CERTAIN

A prophet came to convert the inhabitants of the city. At first people listened to his sermons, but soon they drifted away till there was not a single soul to hear the prophet when he spoke.

One day a traveller said to him, "Why do you go on preaching?"

Said the prophet, "In the beginning I hoped to change these people. If I still go on shouting it is to keep them from changing me."

RIVER WATER FOR SALE

*The Master's sermon consisted
of one enigmatic sentence.*

*With a wry smile he said, "All
I do is sit on the river bank
selling river water."*

I was so busy buying the water that I failed to see
the river.

THE MEDAL

A mother could not get her son to
come home before sunset. So, she told
him that the road to their house was
haunted by ghosts who came out after dusk.

By the time the boy grew up he was so afraid
of ghosts that he refused to run errands at
night. So she gave him a medal and taught
him that it would protect him.

Bad religion gives him faith in the medal.
Good religion gets him to see that ghosts do not exist.

NASRUDDIN IN CHINA

*Mulla Nasruddin went to China.
There he gathered a group of
disciples to prepare them for
enlightenment. When they became
enlightened, they stopped
coming to his lectures!*

It is no credit to your Guru that you sit at his feet
forever.

THE GURU'S CAT

*Each time the guru sat for worship
with his students the ashram cat would
come in to distract them, so he ordered
them to tie it when the ashram was at prayer.*

*After the guru died the cat
continued to be tied at worship time.
And when the cat expired, another cat
was brought into the ashram to make sure
that the guru's orders were faithfully
observed at worship time.*

*Centuries passed and learned treatises
were written by the guru's scholarly disciples
on the liturgical significance of tying up a
cat while worship is performed.*

LITURGICAL VESTMENTS

October, 1917: The Russian Revolution is born. History takes a new direction.

The story goes that the Russian Church was assembled in Council that very month. A passionate debate arose about the colour of a certain liturgical vestment. Some wanted white. Other purple.

Coming to grips with a Revolution is more of a bother than organizing a Liturgy. I'd rather say my prayers than get involved in neighbourhood disputes.

DANDELIONS

A man who took great pride in his lawn
found himself with a large crop of dandelions.
He tried every method he knew
to destroy them. Still they plagued him.

Finally he wrote the Department of Agriculture.
He enumerated all the things
he had tried and closed his letter with
the question: "What shall I do now?"

In due course the reply came: "We suggest
you learn to love them."

I was proud of my lawn but I too was plagued with
dandelions that I kept fighting with every means in
my power. So learning to love them was no easy
task.

I began by talking to them each day. Cordial. Friendly. They maintained a sullen silence. They were smarting from the war I had waged against them – and were suspicious of my motives.

But the day came when they smiled. And relaxed. And we started to be friends.

My lawn, of course, was ruined. But how attractive my garden became!

* * * * * * *

He was becoming blind by degrees. And he fought it with every means in his power. When medicine gave out, he fought it with his emotions. It took courage to say, "I suggest you learn to love you blindness."

At first he would have nothing to do with it. And when he eventually brought himself to speak to his blindness his words were bitter. But he kept on speaking till the bitterness became resignation and tolerance and acceptance and, one day, much to his own surprise, friendliness... and love. Then came the day when he was able to put his arm around his blindness and say, "I love you." That was the day I saw him smile again.

His vision, of course, was lost forever. But how attractive his face became!

DON'T CHANGE

I was a neurotic for years. Anxious, depressed, selfish. And everyone kept telling me to change.

And I resented them, and agreed with them, and wanted to change, but simply couldn't, no matter how I tried.

66

What hurt the most was that, like the others, my closest friend kept urging me to change. So I felt powerless and trapped.

One day he said "Don't change. I love you as you are."

Those words were music to my ears: "Don't change. Don't change. Don't change... I love you as you are."

I relaxed. I came alive. And, suddenly, I changed!

Now I know that I couldn't really change till I found someone to love me whether I changed or not.

Is this how you love me, God?

MY FRIEND

Malik, son of Dinar, was upset about the profligate behaviour of a youth who lived text door. For a long time he did nothing, hoping someone else would intervene. But when the youth's behaviour became intolerable Malik went to him and insisted that he change his ways.

The youth calmly replied he was a protegé of the Sultan, so no one could prevent him from living as he wished.

Said Malik, "I shall personally complain to the Sultan." Said the youth, "That will be a waste of time because the Sultan will not change his mind."

"I shall then denounce you to Allah," Malik said. "Allah," said the youth, "is far too forgiving to condemn me."

Malik went away defeated. But when the young man's reputation got so bad that there was a public outcry, Malik felt it was his duty to rebuke him. On the way to his house, he heard a Voice that said, "Do not touch my friend. He is under my protection." Malik was thrown into confusion and, when he got to the presence of the youth, did not know what to say.

Said the young man, "What have you come for now?" Said Malik, "I came to reprimand you. But on my way here a Voice instructed me to let you be for you are under His protection."

The profligate seemed stunned. "Did he say I was His friend?" he asked. But by then Malik had already left. Years later Malik met the man in Mecca. He had been so touched by the words of the Voice that he had given up his possessions and become a wandering mendicant. "I have come here in search of my Friend," he said to Malik, and died.

God, the friend of a sinner! A statement as dangerous as it is effective. I tried it on myself one day. I said, "God is far too forgiving to condemn me." And I suddenly heard the Good News—for the first time in my life.

THE ARAB ASPIRANT

The Arab Master Jalal-ud-din Rumi would enjoy telling this story:

One day Mohammed was offering morning prayer at the Mosque. Among the crowd of people praying with the Prophet was an Arab aspirant.

Mohammed began to read the Koran and recited the verse in which Pharaoh makes the claim, "I am your true God." On hearing this the good aspirant, in an outburst of spontaneous indignation, shouted: "The boastful son of a bitch!"

The Prophet said nothing, but after prayer was over the others began to rebuke the Arab: "You ought to be ashamed of yourself! Your prayer has surely displeased God for not only did you interrupt the holy silence but you also used filthy language in the presence of God's Prophet".

The poor Arab trembled with fear until Gabriel appeared to the Prophet and said: "God sends greetings to you and wishes you to get these people to stop scolding that simple Arab; indeed his spontaneous profanity moved my heart more than the holy prayers of the others."

70

WE ARE THREE, YOU ARE THREE

When his ship stopped at a remote island for a day, the bishop determined to use the time as profitably as possible. He strolled along the seashore and came across three fishermen attending to their nets. In pidgin English they announced to him that centuries before they had been Christianized by missionaries. "We Christian!" they said, proudly pointing to one another.

The bishop was impressed. Did they know the Lord's Prayer? They had never heard of it. The bishop was shocked.

"What do you say, then, when you pray?"

"We lift eyes in heaven. We pray, 'We are three, you are three, have mercy on us.'" The bishop was appalled at the primitive, the downright heretical, nature of the prayer. So he spent the whole day teaching them the Lord's Prayer. The fishermen were poor learners, but they gave it all they had and before the bishop sailed away next day he had the satisfaction of hearing them go through the formula faultlessly.

Months later his ship happened to pass by those islands again and the bishop, as he paced the deck reciting evening prayer, recalled with pleasure the three men on that

71

distant island who were now able to pray, thanks to his patient efforts.

Suddenly he saw a spot of light in the east that kept approaching the ship and, as he gazed in wonder, he saw three figures walking on the water. The captain stopped the boat and everyone leaned over the rails to see this sight.

They were the bishop's fishermen, of course. "Bishop," they exclaimed, "We hear your boat go past and come hurry hurry meet you."

"What is it you want?" asked the awestricken bishop.

"Bishop," they said, "We so, so sorry. We forget lovely prayer. We say: Our Father in heaven, holy be your name, your kingdom come... then we forget. Tell us prayer again."

It was a chastened bishop who replied, "Go back to your homes, my friends, and each time you pray, say, 'We are three, you are three, have mercy on us!'

PRAYER CAN BE DANGEROUS

Here is a favourite of the Sufi Master Sa'di of Shiraz:

A friend of mine was delighted that his wife was pregnant. He ardently desired a male child. And he made vows to God with this in mind.

His wife gave birth to a boy. My friend rejoiced and threw a party for the entire village.

Years later, on my return from Mecca, I passed through the village of my friend and was told he was in jail.

"What happened?" I asked.

"His son got drunk, killed a man and ran away. So his father has been thrown into prison."

To persistently ask God for what we want is laudable–and perilous.

NARADA

Narada the Hindu sage was on a pilgrimage to the temple of Lord Vishnu. He was given hospitality one night in the hut of a childless couple. Before he set out again the man said to Narada, "You are going to worship Vishnu. Tell him to give me a child."

Narada said to the Lord, "Be merciful to that man and give him a child." The Lord replied, with an air of finality, "It is not in the destiny of that man to have children." So Narada performed his devotions and went back home.

Five years later he was on pilgrimage again and was again given shelter by the hospitable couple. This time two little children were playing at the door of the hut.

"Whose children are these?" said Narada. "Mine," said the man.

Narada was intrigued. The man went on, "After you left us, five years ago, a sannyasi came to our village. We put him up for the night and next day, before he departed, he blessed my wife and me... and these are the fruits of his blessing."

When Narada got to the temple next day, he shouted from the forecourt, "Did you not tell me it was not in the destiny of that man to have children? He has two!"

The Lord laughed aloud when he heard this. "That must be the doing of a saint," he said. "Saints have the power to change destiny!"

As they discovered at a wedding feast when the mother of Jesus got him to work a miracle before his destiny allowed it.

DESTINY IN A TOSSED COIN

The Japanese General Nabunaga decided to attack even though he had only one soldier to the enemy's ten. He was sure he would win, but his soldiers were full of fear.

On the way to battle they stopped at a Shinto shrine. After praying in the shrine Nabunaga came out and said, "I shall now toss a coin. If it is heads, we shall win. If tails, we shall lose. Destiny will now reveal herself."

He tossed the coin. It was heads. The soldiers were so keyed up for the fight that they wiped out the enemy.

Next day an aide said to Nabunaga, "No one can change Destiny."

"Right," said Nabunaga showing him a doubled coin that was heads on both sides.

Who makes Destiny?

PRAYING FOR RAIN

When the neurotic comes for help, he rarely wants
to be healed, for healing is a painful thing. What
he really wants is to be made comfortable in his
neurosis. Often he is looking for a miracle–a
painless cure.

*The old man dearly loved his after-dinner
pipe. One night his wife smelled
something burning and shouted,
"For heavens' sake, Pa! You've
set your whiskers on fire."*

*"I know it," answered the old man
angrily. 'Can't you see I'm praying
for rain?"*

THE DISABLED FOX

A fable of the Arab mystic Sa'di:

> *A man walking through the forest saw a fox
> that had lost its legs and wondered how it
> lived. Then he saw a tiger come with game
> in its mouth. The tiger had his fill and
> left the rest for the fox.*

> *The next day too God sent the tiger to
> feed the fox. The man began to wonder
> at God's greatness and thought, "I too
> shall lie in a corner trusting the
> Lord to give me all I need."*

> *He did this for a month, and was almost
> at death's door when he heard a Voice
> that said, "O you who are on the path
> of error, open your eyes to the Truth!
> Imitate the tiger not the fox."*

On the street I saw a naked child, hungry and
shivering in the cold. I became angry and said to
God, "Why do you allow this? Why don't you do
something?"

God did not reply. That night he said, quite
suddenly, "I certainly did something. I made you."

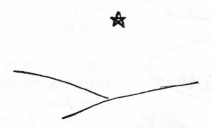

THE FOOD GOD

God decided to visit the earth
so He sent an angel to survey
the place before his visit.

The angel brought back this report:
"Most of them are starving and
most of them are unemployed."

God said, "Then I shall become
incarnate in the form of food
for the hungry and work for the
unemployed."

THE FIVE MONKS

The Lama of the South sent a request to the Great Lama of the North for a wise and holy monk to train the novices. To everyone's astonishment, the Great Lama sent five monks instead of one. To those who enquired he said, cryptically, "We will be lucky if one of them gets to the Lama."

The group had been on the road some days when a messenger came running up to them and said, "The priest of our village has died. We need someone to take his place." The village seemed a pleasant place and the priest's salary was princely. One of the monks was seized with pastoral concern. "I should not be a Buddhist," he said, "If I did not serve these people." So he dropped out.

80

Some days later they were at the palace of a king who took a fancy to one of them. "Stay with us," said the king, "and you shall marry my daughter. And when I die, you will be king." The monk was drawn to the lustre of the throne, so he said, "What better way to influence the people of this kingdom than to be king? I should not be a Buddhist if I did not seize this chance to serve the interests of religion." He too dropped out.

One night, in a hilly region, the monks came to the solitary hut of a pretty girl who gave them hospitality and thanked God for their presence. Her parents had been killed by mountain bandits and the girl was all alone and very fearful. Next day, when it was time to leave, one of the monks declared, "I shall stay on here. I should not be a Buddhist if I did not show compassion to this girl."

The remaining two finally came to a Buddhist village and were scandalized to find that the inhabitants had abandoned their religion under the influence of a Hindu theologian. One of the monks said, "I owe it to these people and to the Lord Buddha himself to win them back to the faith."

The fifth monk eventually got to the Lama of the South.

I have always dropped out for the best of reasons: to reform the liturgy, to change Church structures, to update the study of scripture and to make theology relevant. Religious activity is my favourite escape from God.

THE JOB

Enter the first applicant.

*"You understand that this is a simple test
we are giving you before we offer you the
job you have applied for?"*
"Yes."
"Well, what is two plus two?"
"Four."

Enter the second applicant.

"Are you ready for the test?"
"Yes."
"Well, what is two plus two?"
"Whatever the boss says it is."

The second applicant got the job.

Which comes first, orthodoxy or the truth?

DIOGENES

The philosopher Diogenes was dining on bread and lentils. He was seen by the philosopher Aristippus who lived in considerable comfort by fawning on the king.

Said Aristippus, "Learn subservience to the king and you will not live on lentils."

Said Diogenes, "Learn to live on lentils and you will not have to cultivate the king."

83

STAND UP AND BE COUNTED

When Krushchev pronounced his famous denunciation of Stalin, someone in the Congress Hall is reported to have said, "Where were you, Comrade Krushchev, when all those innocent people were being slaughtered?"

Krushchev paused, looked round the Hall, and said, "Will the person who said that kindly stand up!"

Tension mounted in the Hall. No one moved.

Said Krushchev, "Well, whoever you are, you have your answer now. I was in exactly the same position then as you find yourself in now."

THE TRUTH SHOP

I could hardly believe my eyes when I saw the name of the shop: THE TRUTH SHOP.

The salesgirl was very polite: What type of truth did I wish to purchase, partial or whole? The whole truth, of course. No deceptions for me, no defences, no rationalizations. I wanted my truth plain and unadulterated. She waved me on to another side of the store.

The salesman there pointed to the price tag. "The price is very high, sir," he said. "What is it?" I asked, determined to get the whole truth, no matter what it cost. "Your security, sir," he answered.

I came away with a heavy heart. I still need the safety of my unquestioned beliefs.

THE NARROW PATH

*God warned the people of an earthquake
that would swallow up the waters of the land.
The water that replaced them would make
everyone insane.*

*Only the prophet took God seriously. He
saved up a supply of water in his mountain
cave to last him till he died.*

Sure enough, the earthquake came, the water vanished and new water filled the streams and lakes and rivers. A few months later the prophet came down to the plains. Everyone had indeed gone mad, and attacked him, for they thought it was he who was insane.

So the prophet went back to his mountain cave, glad for the water he had saved. But he could not bear his loneliness so he went down to the plains once more. Again he was rejected by the people for he was so unlike them.

The prophet then succumbed. He threw away the water he had saved, drank the new water with the people and became one with them in their insanity.

The way to Truth is narrow. You always walk alone.

THE PHONY

It was some sort of New Religion. The hall was packed mostly with elderly ladies. One of the speakers was dressed in nothing more than a turban and a loincloth. He spoke, feelingly, of the power of Mind over Matter.

Everyone listened spellbound. The speaker eventually returned to his place right in front of me. His neighbour turned to him and asked in a loud whisper, "Do you really believe what you said, that the body feels nothing at all and it's all in the mind?"

"Of course I do," said the phony with pious conviction.

"Then" said his neighbour. "Would you mind changing places with me? I'm sitting in a draught."

Why do I try to practise what I preach? If I stuck to preaching what I practise I'd be less of a phony.

THE DREAM CONTRACT

Nasruddin was fast asleep at nine in the morning. The sun was in the sky, the birds were singing in the trees and his breakfast was getting cold. So his wife decided to wake him.

He woke up in a rage. "Why did you wake me up just now?" he yelled.

"The sun has risen in the sky," said she, "the birds are singing in the trees and your breakfast is getting cold."

"Breakfast be damned," he said, "I was about to sign a contract worth a million grammes of gold!"

With that he closed his eyes to recapture his shattered dream and those million grammes of gold.

Now Nasruddin was cheating in that contract and his business partner was a tyrant.

If, on recapturing the dream, he stops his cheating, he will become a saint.

If he struggles to free the people from the oppression of the tyrant he will be a freedom fighter.

If, in the middle of it all, he suddenly realizes he is dreaming, he will become Awakened. Enlightened.

What kind of saint or freedom fighter are you if you are still asleep?

VERY WELL, VERY WELL

A village girl became an unwed mother and, after several beatings, revealed who the father was: the Zen Master living on the outskirts of the village.

The villagers trooped into the Master's house, rudely disturbed his meditation, denounced him as a hypocrite and told him to keep the baby. All the Master said was, "Very well. Very well."

He picked the baby up and made arrangements with the woman next door to look after it at his expense.

His name, of course, was ruined, and his disciples all abandoned him.

When this had gone on for a year, the girl could bear it no longer and confessed that she had lied. The father was the boy next door.

The villagers bowed profoundly to the Master to beg his pardon and ask to take the baby back. And all the Master said as he handed back the child was, "Very well. Very well."

The Awakened man!

91

SONS DEAD IN A DREAM

*A fisherman and his wife got a son
after many years of marriage. The boy
was his parents' pride and joy. Then,
one day, he became seriously ill and,
though a fortune was spent on medicines,
he died.*

*The mother was broken-hearted. There
wasn't a tear in the father's eyes.*

*When his wife reproached him for his
lack of sorrow, the fisherman said,
"Let me tell you why I do not weep.
Last night I dreamt I was a king and
the father of eight sturdy boys. Then
suddenly I woke up. Now I am greatly
puzzled: Should I weep for those
boys or for this one?"*

THE GOLDEN EAGLE

A man found an eagle's egg and placed it under a brooding hen. The eaglet hatched with the chickens and grew to be like them. He clucked and cackled; scratched the earth for worms; flapped his wings and managed to fly a few feet in the air.

Years passed. One day, the eagle, now grown old, saw a magnificent bird above him in the sky. It glided in graceful majesty against the powerful wind, with scarcely a movement of its golden wings.

Spellbound, the eagle asked, "Who's that?"

"That's the king of the birds, the eagle," said his neighbour. "He belongs to the sky. We belong to earth–we're chickens."

So the eagle lived and died a chicken for that's what he thought he was.

THE DUCKLING

The Sufi saint, Shams-e Tabrizi tells the following story about himself:

I have been considered a misfit since my childhood days. No one seemed to understand me. My own father once said to me, "You are not crazy enough to be put in a madhouse, and not withdrawn enough to be put in a monastery. What shall I do with you?"

I replied, "A duck's egg was put under a hen. When the egg hatched the duckling walked with the hen to the edge of a pool and went straight into the water. The poor hen stayed anxiously clucking on land. Now, dear father, I have walked into the Ocean and find in it my home. Am I to blame if you choose to stay on shore?"

94

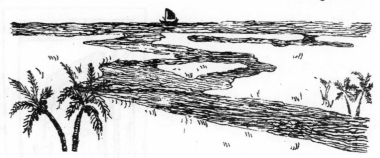

THE SALT DOLL

A salt doll journeyed for thousands
of miles and stopped on the edge of
the sea.

It was fascinated by this moving
liquid mass, so unlike anything it
had seen before.

"What are you?" said the salt doll
to the sea.

"Come in and see," said the sea with
a smile.

So the doll waded in. The further it
went the more it dissolved till there
was only a pinch of it left. Before
that last bit dissolved, the doll
exclaimed in wonder, "Now I know
what I am!"

WHO AM I?

A tale from Attar of Neishapur

The lover knocked at his Beloved's door.
"Who knocks?" said the Beloved from within.
"It is I," said the lover.
"Go away. This house will not hold you and me."

The lover withdrew and pondered for years on the words the Beloved had said. Then he returned and knocked again.

"Who knocks?"
"It is you."

The door was immediately opened.

THE TALKATIVE LOVER

A lover pressed his suit unsuccessfully for many months, suffering the atrocious pains of rejection. Finally his sweetheart yielded. "Come to such and such a place, at such and such an hour," she said.

So the lover finally found himself seated beside his beloved. He pulled out a sheaf of love letters that he had written to her over the months. They were passionate expressions of pain and burning desire. He began to read them aloud. The minutes passed and he read on and on.

Finally the woman burst out, "What kind of a blockhead are you? Those letters tell of your longing. Well, here I am with you at last, and you are lost in your ludicrous letters."

"Here I am with you," says God, "and you keep thinking of me in your head, talking of me with your tongue, and searching for me in your books. When will you shut up and see?"

DROPPING THE 'I'

> Disciple: *I have come to offer you my service.*
>
> Master: *If you dropped the 'I' service would certainly follow.*

You could give all your goods to feed the poor and your body to be burnt and not have love at all.

Keep your goods and drop the 'I'. Don't burn your body; burn the ego. Love will instantly arise.

DROP YOUR NOTHING

Disciple: *I have come to you with nothing in my hands.*

Master: *Drop it at once!*

Disciple: *But how can I drop it? It is nothing.*

Master: *Then carry it around with you!*

Your *nothing* can be your most valued possession.

THE ZEN MASTER AND THE CHRISTIAN

*A Christian visited a Zen Master
and said, "Allow me to read you
the Sermon on the Mount."*

*"I shall listen with pleasure,"
said the Master.*

*The Christian read a sentence
and looked up. The Master smiled
and said, "Whoever said those words
was truly an Enlightened Man."*

*This pleased the Christian. He
read on. The Master interrupted
and said, "Those words come from
a Saviour of mankind."*

*The Christian was delighted. He
read on to the end. The Master
then declared, "That sermon was
pronounced by someone radiant
with Divinity."*

*The Christian's joy was boundless.
He left, determined to return
another day and persuade the Master
to become a Christian.*

On the way back home he found Jesus standing
by the roadside. "Lord," he said excitedly, "I got
that man to confess you are divine!"

Jesus smiled and said, "And did it do you any good
except inflate your Christian ego?"

COMFORT FOR THE DEVIL

An ancient Christian legend:

When the Son of God was nailed to the Cross and died, he went straight down to hell and set free all the sinners there in torment.

And the Devil wept and wailed for he thought he would get no more sinners for hell.

Then God said to him, "Do not weep, for I shall send you all those who are self-righteous in their condemnation of sinners. And hell will fill up again till I return."

BETTER SLEEP THAN SLANDER

Sadi of Shiraz tells this tale about himself:

*I used to be a pious child, fervent in
prayer and devotion. One night I was
keeping vigil with my father, the Holy
Koran on my lap.*

*The others in the room began to
slumber and soon everyone was
fast asleep, so I said to my father,
"None of these sleepers opens his
eyes or raises his head to say his
prayers. You would think they were
dead."*

*My father replied, "My beloved son,
I would rather wish you too were sleeping
like them than slandering."*

THE MONK AND THE WOMAN

Two Buddhist monks, on their way to the monastery, found an exceedingly beautiful woman at the river bank. Like them, she wanted to cross the river, but the water was too high. So one of them took her across on his shoulders.

The other was thoroughly scandalized. For two hours he scolded the offender for his breach of the Rule: Had he forgotten he was a monk? How had he dared to touch the woman? And worse, carry her over the river? And what would people say? Had he not disgraced their holy Religion? And so on.

The victim took it gamely. At the end of the lecture he said, "Brother, I dropped that woman at the river. Are you carrying her still?"

The Arab mystic, Abu Hassan Bushanja, says, "The act of sinning is not so harmful as the desire and the thought of it. It is one thing for the body to indulge in pleasure for a moment, and quite another for the mind and heart to chew on it endlessly."

Each time I chew on the sins of others, I suspect the chewing gives me greater pleasure than the sinning gives the sinner.

THE SPIRITUAL HEART ATTACK

Uncle Tom had a weak heart, so when the family learnt that he had inherited a billion dollars, they feared to tell him lest the news give him a stroke. So they sought the help of the priest who assured them he would do the needful.

"Tell me, Tom," said Father Murphy, "If God, in his mercy, were to send you a billion dollars, what would you do with them?"

"I'd give you half of it for the Church, Father."

Father Murphy got the stroke!

When an industrialist got a stroke from pushing his industrial empire it was easy to show him his selfishness and greed. When the priest got a stroke from pushing God's Kingdom he could not see that this was selfishness in a more respectable disguise: Is it God's Kingdom you are pushing or yourself? The Kingdom needs no pushing. Your *anxiety* betrays you, does it not?

TO KNOW CHRIST

A dialogue between a recent convert and an unbelieving friend:

> *"So you have been converted to Christ?"*
> *"Yes."*
> *"Then you must know a great deal about him. Tell me: what country was he born in?"*
> *"I don't know."*
> *"What was his age when he died?"*
> *"I don't know."*
> *"How many sermons did he preach?"*
> *"I don't know."*
> *"You certainly know very little for a man who claims to be converted to Christ!"*

"You are right. I am ashamed at how little I know about him. But this much I know: Three years ago I was a drunkard. I was in debt. My family was falling apart. My wife and children would dread my coming home each day. Now I have given up drink; we are out of debt; ours is a happy home. All this Christ has done. This much I know of him!"

To *really* know. That is, to be transformed by what one knows.

THE LOOK OF JESUS

In the gospel according to Luke we read:

But Peter said, "Man, I do not know what you are talking about." At that moment, while he was still speaking, a cock crew; and the Lord turned and looked straight at Peter... and Peter went outside and wept.

I related well with the Lord. I would converse with him, thank him, ask for help.

But always I had this uneasy feeling that he wanted me to look at him... And I would not. I would talk, but look away when I sensed he was looking at me.

I was afraid I should find an accusation in his eyes of some unrepented sin. Or a demand: something he wanted from me.

One day I summoned up courage and looked! There was no accusation. No demand. The eyes just said, "I love you."

And, like Peter, I went outside and wept.

THE GOLDEN EGG

A reading from the Scriptures:

This is what the Lord says: A farmer owned a goose that laid a golden egg each day. His wife, an avaricious woman, could not resign herself to a single egg a day. So she killed the goose in the hope of getting all the eggs at once.

Thus far the Word of God!

An Atheist heard that text and scoffed: A goose that lays golden eggs! It goes to show the absurdity of your Scriptures!

When a religious Scholar read that text, he reacted thus: "The Lord revealed the existence of that goose, so it must be true no matter how absurd it seems. Now you will ask, as well you may, how an egg, while never ceasing to be an egg in every sense, can simultaneously have the properties of gold. Different schools of thought explain it differently. But what is called for here is an act of faith in this mystery that baffles human understanding."

There was even a preacher who, inspired by that text, travelled through towns and villages seriously exhorting the inhabitants to accept the fact that, at some privileged point in human history, God had created golden eggs.

It is better to teach people the evils of avarice than to promote belief in golden eggs.

GOOD NEWS

Jesus began to teach in parables.
He said: The kingdom of God is like
two brothers who were called by God
to give up all they had and serve
humanity.

The older responded to the call though he
had to tear himself away from his fianceé
and his family and go off to a distant land
to spend himself in the service of the poor.
Years later he was imprisoned for his work,
tortured and put to death.

110

And the Lord said, "Well done my good and faithful servant! You gave me a thousand measures of service. I shall now give you a thousand million measures of beatitude. Enter into the joy of your Lord."

The younger boy ignored the call. He married the girl he loved and prospered in his business. He was kind to his wife and children and gave an occasional alms to the poor.

And when he came to die, the Lord said, "Well done my good and faithful servant! You gave me twenty measures of service. I shall now give you a thousand million measures of beatitude. Enter into the joy of your Lord."

When the older boy was told that his brother was to get the same reward as he, he was surprised. And he rejoiced. "Lord," he said, "had I known this at the time you called me I know I would have done exactly what I did for love of you."

JONEYED AND THE BARBER

The holy man Joneyed, dressed in beggar's clothes, entered the barber's shop in Mecca. The barber, who was shaving a nobleman, left his wealthy customer to shave this beggar first. And not only did he not charge him for his services, he even gave him an alms and sent him on his way.

Joneyed was so impressed, he resolved he would hand over to the barber whatever he got in the way of alms that day. It so happened that a well-to-do pilgrim gave him a purse full of gold coins. Overjoyed, he ran to the barber's shop and offered him the purse.

When the barber understood why he was being given the gold, he was enraged. "What kind of a holy man are you," he yelled, "that you come to reward me for an act of love!"

* * * * * * *

A fantasy:

The devotee yells at the Lord, "What kind of a God are you that you dare to reward my devotion!"

The Lord replies with a smile, "I am Love. So how can I offer rewards?"

When you seek a recompense your gift becomes a bribe.

THE ELDER SON

When God walked into heaven and found that everyone was there, he wasn't pleased at all. He owed it to his justice, did he not, to carry out his threats. So everyone was summoned to his throne and the Angel asked to read the Ten Commandments.

The First Commandment was announced. Said God, "All who have broken this Commandment will now betake themselves to hell." And so it was done.

The same was done with each of the other Commandments. By the time the Angel came to read the Seventh, no one was left in heaven except a recluse–smug and self-complacent.

God looked up and thought: "Only one person left in heaven? That makes it very lonesome." So he shouted out, "Come back, everyone!"

When the recluse heard that everyone was forgiven, he yelled in rage, "This is unjust! Why didn't you tell me this before?"

114

THE OLD LADY'S RELIGION

*A very religious-minded old lady
was dissatisfied with all existing
religions, so she founded one
of her own.*

*A reporter, who genuinely wanted
to understand her point of view,
said to her, "Do you really
believe, as people say you do,
that no one will go to heaven
except you and your housemaid?"*

*The old lady pondered the question
carefully and said, "Well, I'm not
so sure of Mary."*

LOVE'S FORGETFULNESS

*"Why do you keep talking about
my past mistakes?" said the husband.
"I thought you had forgiven and forgotten."*

*"I have, indeed," said the wife.
"But don't you ever forget that
I have forgiven and forgotten."*

*   *   *   *   *   *   *

Sinner: *"Remember not my sins,
oh Lord,!"*

Lord: *What sins? I forgot them
long ago. You'll have to
prod my memory.*

Love keeps no record of wrongs. (1 Cor. 13)

THE LOTUS

The Guru wanted his disciples to wear a special garb that would show the world their consecration. He called it *giving witness.*

> *I saw a lotus in a pond and said,*
> *"How beautiful you are, my dear!*
> *And how beautiful must be the God*
> *who made you!"*

> *And the lotus blushed. She was the*
> *lovelier for being so unconscious*
> *of her beauty.*

> *At another pond I found a lotus*
> *preening her petals to catch my*
> *eye. "Look at my beauty," she*
> *seemed to say, "and glorify my Maker."*

> *I walked on in disgust.*

When I set out to *edify,* I seek to impress—and become a well-intentioned Pharisee!

THE TURTLE

The Emperor of China sent ambassadors to a hermit living in the northern mountains. They were to invite him to become Prime Minister of the Kingdom.

After many days of travel the ambassadors arrived. The hermitage was empty! But nearby in the middle of a river was a half-naked man, seated on a rock, fishing with a line. Could this be the man the Emperor thought so highly of? Enquires at the village proved it was. So they returned to the river bank and, as respectfully as they could, attempted to attract the fisherman's attention.

The hermit waded through the river and stood before the messengers barefoot, arms akimbo.

"What is it you want?"

"Honoured sir, His Majesty the Emperor of China, having heard of your wisdom and your holiness has sent us with these gifts. He invites you to accept the post of Prime Minister of the Realm."

"Prime Minister of the Realm?"

"Yes, respected sir."

"Me?"

"Yes, respected sir."

"Is His Majesty out of his mind?" said the hermit as he roared with uncontrollable laughter to the discomfiture of the ambassadors.

When he was able to control himself, the hermit said, *"Tell me—is it true that mounted over the main altar of the Emperor's chapel is a stuffed turtle whose shell is encrusted with sparkling diamonds?"*

"It is, venerable sir."

"And is it true that once a day the Emperor and his household gather to do homage to this diamond-decorated turtle?"

"It is, sir."

"Now take this turtle here, wagging his tail in the muck. Do you think this little fellow would change places with the turtle in the palace?"

"No, he would not."

"Then go, tell the Emperor that neither would I. For no one can be alive on a pedestal."

BAYAZID BREAKS THE RULE

Bayazid, the Moslem saint, would sometimes deliberately act against the outward forms and rituals of Islam.

It once happened that, on his way back from Mecca, he stopped at the Iranian town of Rey. The townsfolk, who revered him, rushed to make him welcome and created a great stir in the town. Bayazid, who was quite tired of this adulation, waited till he reached the market place. There he bought a loaf of bread and began to munch it in full view of his followers. It was a day of fasting in the month of Ramazan but Bayazid knew that his journey justified the breaking of the law.

Not so his followers. They were so shocked at his behaviour that they promptly left him and went back to their homes. Bayazid impishly remarked to a disciple, "Did you see how the moment I did something contrary to their expectation, their veneration vanished?"

The price you pay for veneration is conformity.

STREAKY PEOPLE

*A preacher put this question to
a class of children: "If all good
people were white and all bad
people black, what colour would
you be?"*

*Little Mary Jane replied: "I'd be
streaky!"*

So would the Preacher. So would the Mahatmas,
Popes and saints.

*A man, looking for a good church to
attend, happened to enter one in which
the people and the priest were reading
from their Prayer Book: "We have left
undone those things which we ought to
have done, and we have done those things
which we ought not to have done."*

*The man dropped into a seat and sighed,
"Thank goodness, I've found my crowd
at last."*

Attempts to hide your streakiness will sometimes
be successful, always dishonest.

MUSIC TO THE DEAF

I used to be deaf. I would
see people stand up and go
through strange gyrations.
They called it dancing. To
me it looked absurd–until
one day I heard the music!

I fail to understand why saints–and lovers–behave the way they do. So I'm waiting for my heart to come alive.

RICHES

Husband: "I'm going to work hard, and some day we are going to be rich."

Wife: "We are rich already, dear, for we have each other. Some day we may have money."

THE CONTENTED FISHERMAN

The industrialist was horrified to find the fisherman lying beside his boat, smoking a pipe.

"Why aren't you out fishing?" said the industrialist.

"Because I have caught enough fish for the day."

"Why don't you catch some more?"

"What would I do with it?"

"Earn more money. Then you could have a motor fixed to your boat and go into deeper waters and catch more fish. That would bring you money to buy nylon nets, so more fish, more money. Soon you would have enough to buy two boats... even a fleet of boats. Then you could be rich like me."

"What would I do then?"

"Then you could really enjoy life."

"What do you think I am doing now?"

Which would you rather have: a fortune or a capacity for enjoyment.

THE SEVEN JARS OF GOLD

A barber was passing under a haunted tree when he heard a voice say, "Would you like to have the seven jars of gold?" He looked around and saw no one. But his greed was aroused, so he shouted eagerly, 'Yes, I certainly would." "Then go home at once." said the voice. "You will find them there."

The barber ran all the way home. Sure enough, there were the seven jars—all full of gold, except for one that was only half-full. Now the barber could not bear the thought of having a half-filled jar. He felt a violent urge to fill it or he simply would not be happy.

So he had all the jewellery of his family melted into coins and thrown into the half-filled jar. But the jar remained as half-filled as before. This was exasperating! He saved and skimped and starved himself and his family. To no avail. No matter how much gold he put into the jar it always stayed half-filled.

*One day he got the King to double his salary.
So the fight to fill the jar was on again. He
even took to begging. The jar devoured each
piece of gold that was flung into it, but
stubbornly refused to fill.*

*The King now noticed how starved the barber
looked. "What's wrong with you?" he asked.
"You used to be so happy when your salary
was smaller. Now it has been doubled and you
are worn out and dejected. Can it be that you
have been given the seven jars of gold?"*

*The barber was astonished. "Who told you
this, Your Majesty?" he asked.*

*The King laughed. "But these are obviously the
symptoms of the person to whom the ghost has
given the seven jars. He once offered them to
me. When I asked if the money could be spent
or was merely to be hoarded he vanished
without a word. That money can't be spent. It
only brings with it the compulsion to hoard. Go
return it to the ghost this minute and you will
be a happy man again."*

A PARABLE ON MODERN LIFE

*The animals met in assembly and began
to complain that humans were always
taking things away from them.*

*"They take my milk," said the cow.
"They take my eggs," said the hen.
"They take my flesh for bacon," said
the hog. "They hunt me for my oil,"
said the whale.*

*The snail was the last to speak.
"I have something they would certainly
take away from me if they could. Something
they want more than anything else.
I have time."*

You have all the time in the world if you would give
it to yourself. What's stopping you?

HOFETZ CHAIM

*In the last century, a tourist from
the States visited the famous Polish
rabbi, Hofetz Chaim.*

*He was astonished to see that the
rabbi's home was only a simple room
filled with books. The only furniture
was a table and a bench.*

*"Rabbi, where is your furniture?"
asked the tourist.*

"Where is yours?" said Hofetz.

*"Mine? But I'm passing through. I'm
only a visitor here.'*

"So am I."

THE SKY AND THE CROW

A tale from the Bhagawat Purana:

A crow once flew into the sky
with a piece of meat in its beak. Twenty other
crows set out in hot pursuit and began
to attack it viciously.

When the crow finally dropped
the meat, its pursuers left it alone and flew
off shrieking after the morsel.

Said the crow: "I've lost the meat
and gained this peaceful sky."

Said a Zen monk,

"When my house burnt down
I got an unobstructed view
of the moon at night!

WHO CAN STEAL THE MOON?

*The Zen Master Ryokan lived a very
frugal life at the foot of a mountain.
One night when the Master was away,
a thief broke into his hut only to discover
there was nothing there to steal.*

*Ryokan returned and caught the burglar.
'You have put yourself to much trouble
to visit me," he said. 'You must not go
away empty-handed. Please take my blanket
and clothes as a gift."
The bewildered thief slunk off with the gift.*

*Ryokan sat naked at the door of his hut,
watching the moon in the sky. 'Poor fellow,"'
he said, "I wish I could give him this."*

THE DIAMOND

*When the sannyasi reached the outskirts
of the village and settled under a tree
for the night, a villager came running
up to him and said, "The stone! The stone!
Give me the precious stone!"*

"What stone?" asked the sannyasi.

*"Last night Lord Shiva told me in a dream
that if I went to the outskirts of the
village at dusk a sannyasi would give
me a stone that would make me
rich forever."*

*The sannyasi rummaged in his sack and,
pulling out a stone, he said, 'He probably
meant this one. I found it in the forest
yesterday. Here, it's yours if you want
it."*

*The man gazed at the stone in wonder. It
was the largest diamond in the world–the
size of a man's head.*

*All night he tossed about in bed. At break
of day he woke the sannyasi and said, "Give
me the wealth that makes it possible for you to
give this stone away."*

132

PRAY FOR A CONTENTED MIND

Said the Lord Vishnu to his devotee:
"I am weary of your never-ending petitions.
I shall grant you three requests. Make sure
you choose them carefully because, having
granted them, I shall grant you nothing more."
The elated devotee did not hesitate: "Here
is my first request," he said, "I want
my wife to die so I can marry a better woman."
His wish was immediately granted.

But when friends and relatives gathered
for the funeral and began to recall the
virtues of his wife, the devotee saw he
had been hasty. So he asked the Lord to
bring her back to life.

That left him with just one petition. He
was determined not to make a mistake this
time, for there would be no chance to change it.
He consulted widely. Some advised him to ask
for immortality. But what good was
immortality, said others, if he did not have
good health? And health if he had no money?
And money if he had no friends?

Years passed and he had still not made
his choice: life or health or wealth or
power or love. Finally he said to the
Lord, "Tell me what to ask for."

The Lord laughed when he saw the man's
predicament, and said, "Ask to be content
no matter what you get."

133

THE WORLD FAIR OF RELIGIONS

My friend and I went to the World Fair Of Religions. Not a trade fair. But the competition was fierce, the propaganda loud.

The hand-outs at the Jewish Stall said that God was All-Compassionate and the Jews were his Chosen People. The Jews. No other people were as Chosen as they.

At the Moslem Stall we learnt that God was All-Merciful and Mohammed his only Prophet. Salvation comes from listening of God's Prophet.

The message at the Christian Stall was: God is Love and there is no salvation outside the Church. Join the Church or risk damnation forever.

134

On the way out I asked my friend what he thought of God. He replied, "He's bigoted fanatical and cruel."

Back home, I said to God, "How do you put up with this sort of thing? Don't you see they have been giving you a bad name for centuries?"

God said, "It wasn't I who organized the Fair. In fact, I'd be too ashamed to visit it."

DISCRIMINATION

I went right back to the Religious Fair. This time I heard a speech of the High Priest of the Balakri Religion. The Prophet Balakri, we were told, was the Messiah, born in the fifth century Holy Land of Mesambia.

I had another exchange with God that night. "You're a great Discriminator, aren't you, God? Why does the fifth century have to be the enlightened century and Mesambia the holy land? What's wrong with my century? And my land?"

To which God answered, "A feast day is holy because it shows that every day is holy. And a sanctuary is holy because it indicates the holiness of every spot on earth. So the Messiah is called the Son of God to show that everyone is divine."

JESUS AT THE FOOTBALL MATCH

*Jesus Christ said he had never been
to a football match. So we took him
to one, my friends and I. It was a
ferocious battle between the Protestant
Punchers and the Catholic Crusaders.*

*The Crusaders scored first. Jesus cheered
wildly and threw his hat high up in the air.
Then the Punchers scored. And Jesus
cheered wildly and threw his hat high
up in the air.*

*This seemed to puzzle the man behind us.
He tapped Jesus on the shoulder and
asked, "Which side are you rooting for,
my good man?"*

*"Me?" replied Jesus, all excited, "I'm not
rooting for either side. I'm just enjoying
the game."*

*The questioner turned to his neighbour
and sneered, "Hmm, an atheist!"*

We took him up on this after the game. Was he in
the habit of never taking sides? "I side People rather
than Religions," said Jesus, "Human Beings rather
than Sabbath."

RELIGIOUS HATRED

A tourist says to his guide, 'You must be proud of your town. I was especially impressed by the number of Churches in it. Surely the people here must love the Lord."

"Well," says the cynical guide, "they may love the Lord, but they sure as hell hate each other."

Like the little girl who when asked, "Who are pagans?", replied, "Pagans are people who do not fight about religion."

OFFENSIVE AND DEFENSIVE PRAYER

*The Catholic football team was
on its way to an important game.
A reporter boarded the train and
asked for the football coach.*

*"I understand," said the reporter,
"that you carry a chaplain to pray
for the success of the team.
Would you mind introducing me to
him?"*

*"That would be a pleasure," said
the coach. "Which one do you want
to meet, the offensive or the
defensive chaplain?"*

139

IDEOLOGY

Here is a newspaper account of torture practised in modern concentration camps.

*The victim is bound to a metal chair
then electric shocks are administered
to him in increasing intensity till
he confesses.*

*The torturer cups his hands and slaps
the victim on the ear repeatedly till
the eardrum breaks.*

*A dentist straps the prisoner to a
chair and drills till he strikes a
nerve. The drilling goes on till the
victim agrees to cooperate.*

Human beings are not naturally cruel. They become cruel when they are unhappy–or when they succumb to an ideology.

One ideology against another; one religion against another. And people crushed in between them.

The men who crucified Jesus could very well have been gentle husbands and loving fathers who practised cruelty to maintain a religion or an ideology.

If religious people had always followed the instinct of their heart rather than the logic of their religion we would have been spared the sight of heretics burning at stakes, widows walking into funeral pyres and innocent people slaughtered in wars that are waged in the name of God.

Compassion has no ideology.

CHANGE THE WORLD BY CHANGING ME

The Sufi Bayazid says this about himself:
"I was a revolutionary when I was young
and all my prayer to God was: 'Lord give
me the energy to change the world.'"

"As I approached middle age and realized
that half my life was gone without my
changing a single soul, I changed my
prayer to: 'Lord, give me the grace to
change all those who come in contact
with me. Just my family and friends,
and I shall be content.'"

"Now that I am an old man and my days
are numbered, my one prayer is, 'Lord,
give me the grace to change myself.'
If I had prayed for this right from
the start I should not have wasted
my life."

DOMESTICATED REBELS

He was a difficult man. He thought differently and acted differently from the rest of us. He questioned everything. Was he a rebel, a prophet, a psychopath or a hero? "Who can tell the difference?" we said, "And who cares, anyway?"

So we socialized him. We taught him to be sensitive to public opinion and to the feelings of others. We got him to conform. He was a comfortable person to live with now. Well adjusted. We had made him manageable and docile.

We congratulated him on having achieved self conquest. He began to congratulate himself. He did not see that it was we who had conquered him.

*A Big Guy walked into the crowded room
and yelled, "Is there a fellow by the name
of Murphy here?" A Little Fellow stood up
and said, "I'm Murphy."*

*The Big Guy nearly killed him. He cracked
five of his ribs, he broke his nose, he
gave him two black eyes, he flung him in
a heap on the floor. Then he stamped out.*

*After he had gone we were amazed to see
the Little Fellow chuckling to himself.
"I certainly made a fool of that guy."
he was saying softly to himself.
"I'm not Murphy! Ha, ha!"*

A society that domesticates its rebels has gained
its peace. But it has lost its future.

THE LOST SHEEP

A parable for religious educators.

*A sheep found a hole in the fence
and crept through it. He wandered
far and could not find his way back.*

*And then he realized that he was
being followed by a wolf. He ran
and ran, but the wolf kept chasing
him, until the shepherd rescued him
and carried him lovingly back to the
fold.*

*And in spite of everyone's advice
the shepherd refused to nail up
the hole in the fence.*

THE PERFECT APPLE

Nasruddin had barely finished his discourse when one of the scoffers in the crowd said to him, "Instead of spinning spiritual theories, why don't you show us something practical?"

Poor Nasruddin was quite nonplussed. "What kind of practical thing would you want me to show you?" he asked.

Pleased that he had mortified the Mulla and was making an impression on the crowd the scoffer said, "For instance, show us an apple from the garden of Paradise."

Nasruddin immediately picked up an apple and handed it to the man. "But this apple is bad on one side," said the man. "Surely a heavenly apple would be perfect."

"A celestial apple would, indeed, be perfect." said the Mulla, "But given your present faculties, this is as near to a heavenly apple as you will ever get."

Can one expect to see a perfect apple with an imperfect eye?

Or detect goodness in others when one's own heart is selfish?

THE SLAVE GIRL

*A Moslem King fell passionately in love
with a slave girl and had her transferred
from the slave quarters to the palace. He
planned to marry her and make her his
favourite wife but, mysteriously, the girl
fell seriously ill on the very day she
entered the palace.*

*She grew steadily worse. Every known
remedy was given her, to no avail;
she hovered between life and death.*

*In despair the King made an offer of half
his kingdom to anyone who would cure her.
But who would attempt to cure an illness
that had baffled the best physicians of
the realm?*

147

Finally a hakim appeared who asked to be allowed to see the girl alone. After he had spoken with her for an hour he appeared before the throne of the King who anxiously awaited his verdict.

"Your Majesty," said the hakim. "I do indeed have an infallible cure for the girl. And so sure am I of its effectiveness that, were it not to work, I should willingly offer myself to be beheaded. The medicine I propose, however, will prove to be an extremely painful one—not for the girl, but for you.'

"Mention the medicine," shouted the King. "And it shall be given her, no matter the cost."

The hakim looked at the King with compassion and said, "The girl is in love with one of your servants. Give her permission to marry him and she will be instantly cured."

Poor King! He wanted the girl too much to let her go. He loved her too much to let her die.

CONFUCIUS THE SAGE

Pu Shang once said to Confucius, "What
king of sage are you that you can say
that Yen Hui excels you in straight-
forwardness? That in clarifying things
Tuan-mu Tz'u is superior to you? That
Chung Yu is more courageous than you?
And that Chuan-sun is more dignified
than you?"

In his eagerness to get a reply Pu
Shang moved to the edge of the mat
and nearly fell off it. "If these things
are true," he said, "then why are these
four men your disciples?"

*Confucius replied, "Stay right where
you are and I shall tell you. Yen Hui
knows how to be straight-forward, but
he does not know how to be flexible.
Tuan-mu Tz'u knows how to clarify
things, but he does not know how to
give a simple Yes or No for answer.
Chung Yu knows how to be courageous,
but he does not know how to be
cautious. Chuan-sun Shih knows how to be
dignified, but he does not know how to
be unassuming. This is why these four
men are glad to study under me."*

The Moslem, Jalal-ud-din Rumi, says, "A hand that
is always open or always closed is a crippled hand.
A bird that cannot open and close its wings cannot
fly."

O HAPPY FAULT!

*The Jewish mystic Baal Shem had a
curious way of praying to God.
"Remember, Lord," he would say,
"You need me just as much as I
need you. If you did not exist,
whom would I pray to? If I did
not exist, who would do the
praying?"*

It brought me joy to think that if I had not sinned
God would have had no occasion to be forgiving.

THE COCONUT

*A monkey on a tree hurled a coconut
at the head of a Sufi.*

*The man picked it up, drank the
milk, ate the flesh and made a
bowl from the shell.*

Thank you for your criticism of me.

THE SINGER'S VOICE FILLS THE HALL

Overheard outside a concert hall:

"What a singer! His voice filled the hall."

*"Yes, several of us had to leave the hall
to make room for it!"*

*   *   *   *   *   *   *

Overheard in a spiritual counselling session:

*"How can I love God as the Scriptures tell
us to? How can I give Him my whole heart?"*

*"You must first empty your heart of all
created things."*

153

Misleading ! Don't be afraid to fill your heart with the people and things you love, for the love of God won't occupy space in your heart any more than a singer's voice occupies space in a hall.

* * * * * * *

Love is not like a loaf of bread. If I give a chunk of the loaf to you I have less to offer to others. Love is like eucharistic bread: I receive the whole Christ— and so do you; and the next person; and the next.

You can love your mother with your whole heart; and your spouse; and every one of your children. And the wonder is that each stands to gain because love improves in quality each time the heart is given to another person.

If a friend loves you alone and no one else, you would be wise to urge him to give his heart to others for, unless he does this, it is a feeble (and hungry!) heart he offers you.

THANKS AND YES

How does one love God? Certainly not the way one loves the persons one sees and hears and touches. For God is not a *person* in our sense of the word. He is the Unknown, the wholly Other, above terms like *he* and *she; person* and *thing.*

When we say an audience fills the hall and a singer's voice fills the hall, we use the same word, *fill,* to refer to two distinct realities. When we say we love God and we love our friends, we are using the same word, *love,* to express two distinct realities. The singer's voice does not really *fill* the hall; and we cannot really *love* God in the ordinary sense of the word.

To love God with one's whole heart means to say a wholehearted Yes to life; to accept without reservations all that God has ordained for it; to have the attitude that Jesus had when he said, "Not my will, but yours be done."

The finest formulation of what it means to love God totally is found in Dag Hammarsjold's words:

> *For all that has been, Thanks.*
> *To all that shall be, Yes.*

This is the kind of thing one can give to God alone. In this he has no rivals. To understand that this is what it means to love God, is to see at once that it doesn't come in the way to loving your friends wholeheartedly, passionately.

The singer's voice remains in undisputed possession of the crowded hall. The crowd is not a rival to it. The only rival is another voice. God holds undisputed sway over your heart. The people in it are no rivals. The only rival is a person or a thing that causes you to weaken your attitude of *Yes* and *Thanks.*

SIMON PETER

A dialogue from the gospels:

"And you,: said Jesus,
"Who do you say I am?"

Simon Peter answered, "You are the Son of the
Living God."

Then Jesus said, "Simon, son of Jonah, you
are favoured indeed! You did not learn
that from mortal man: my Father revealed it to
you."

A dialogue from life:

Jesus: And you, who do you say I am?

Christian: You are the Son of the living God.

Jesus: Right. But how unfortunate you are that
                 you learnt this only from mortal man.
                 It has not yet been revealed to you by
                 my Father.

Christian: True, Lord. I feel cheated. Somebody
                 gave me the answers before your
                 Father could speak. I marvel at your
                 wisdom that you said nothing to
                 Simon yourself, till your Father had
                 spoken first.

THE SAMARITAN WOMAN

The woman put down her water jar and went off to the town. She said to the people, "Come and see the man who has told me everything I ever did. Could this be the Messiah?"

Christian:
Oh for a teacher like that woman ! She gave no answers. She only asked a question. It must have been tempting to give the answer because she got it from you directly when you said, "I am the Messiah. I who am talking to you."

158

*Many more became disciples because of
what they heard from his own lips. They
said to the woman, 'It is no longer because
of what you said that we believe, for we
have heard him ourselves, and we know that
this is, indeed, the Saviour of the world.*

Christian:

I have been content, Lord, to learn about you at
second hand. From Scriptures and saints;
preachers and popes. I wish I could say to them
all, "It is no longer because of what you said that I
believe, for I have heard him myself."

IGNATIUS OF LOYOLA

The sixteenth century mystic, Ignatius of Loyola, said that at the time of his conversion he had no one to turn to for guidance, so the Lord Himself taught him the way a schoolmaster teaches a child. He once declared that even if all the scriptures were destroyed, he would hold on to what they revealed because of what the Lord had taught him personally.

160

Christian:

I have, unfortunately, had a surfeit of
people to guide me. They badgered me
with their persistent teachings till I
could barely hear you through the din.
I never thought I could have *you*
for my teacher, for they said, "We are
all the teachers you have; he who
listens to us, listens to Him."

But I am wrong to blame them or deplore
their presence in my life. It is I who
am to blame. For I lacked the firmness
to silence them; the courage to find
out for myself; the patience to wait
for your appointed time; and the trust
that someday, somewhere, you would
break your silence and reveal yourself
to me.